my first
Juices
& Smoothies

NOTES

Standard level spoon and cup measurements have been used in all recipes unless otherwise indicated.

This book should not be considered as a replacement for professional medical treatment; a physician should be consulted on all matters relating to health. While the advice and information in this book is believed to be accurate, neither the author nor the publisher can accept any legal responsibility for any illness sustained while following the advice in this book.

An Hachette UK company
www.hachette.co.uk

First published in Great Britain in 2007 by Hamlyn, a division of Octopus Publishing Group Limited, Endeavour House, 189 Shaftesbury Avenue, London WC2H 8JY
www.octopusbooksusa.com

Revised edition published in 2014.

Distributed in the US by Hachette Book Group USA, 237 Park Avenue New York NY 10017 USA

Distributed in Canada by Canadian Manda Group, 165 Dufferin Street Toronto, Ontario, Canada M6K 3H6

ISBN 978-0-600-62967-2

Printed and bound in China.

10 9 8 7 6 5 4 3 2 1

my *first*
Juices
& Smoothies

HEALTHY RECIPES CHILDREN WILL LOVE

AMANDA CROSS

Contents

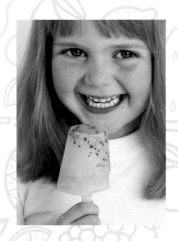

Introduction

Do your kids refuse cabbage and turn their noses up at broccoli? Would they prefer to have a cookie rather than eat an apple?

Yes? Well, it's all part of the ongoing battle between kids and their parents when it comes to getting them to reach their five-a-day fruit and vegetable quota. They would be much happier digging into an unhealthy package of potato chips or munching a bar of chocolate—after all, they're kids, what else would you expect?

It's no real wonder you have a fight on your hands. Food manufacturers around the the world manipulate your little ones into wanting beverages and snacks that have little or no nutritive value, and in all honesty, they are creating all kinds of health problems in the future for a whole generation of growing, developing children.

Let's face it, to the taste buds of a child, heavily advertised "banana-flavored" junk tends to beat a real banana hands down. It's full of addictive sugars, plenty of sodium, and loads of hydrogenated fats, with a few additives thrown in for good measure. In addition, all the other kids in the playground are eating it, and they might even get one of the six free collectable plastic cartoon characters.

However, that collectable cartoon figure will be long gone by the time they join the growing number of teenagers being diagnosed with diabetes, or when as young adults they find out they have developed cardiac problems or cancer. It certainly won't be able to help them cope with their schoolwork or get a good night's sleep; and when obesity damages their self-confidence and

stops them from participating in physical activities that could help them feel much healthier and better about themselves, they aren't going to derive any comfort from a long-forgotten childhood hero.

This may sound a little harsh but, unfortunately, it is a serious problem that is getting worse. Luckily for many children, however, the adults who care for them are waking up to the reality that what they feed their kids today will have an impact—good or bad— on their tomorrows. With a lot of dedication, some imagination, and a touch of guile, you can improve the situation tremendously. The most

important thing is to start now, because the earlier you can get a child to enjoy fueling their bodies with healthy natural food, the less chance they'll have of developing destructive eating habits that will in time severely compromise their future well-being.

Your first strategy in this battle for good health should be to get them active and get them thirsty, because the delicious juices and smoothies in this book will hit the spot, and instead of the usual refusals, you may even hear them asking for more.

WHY JUICE?

Juicing has to be one of the easiest and most effective ways to make sure your children get to the five-a-day target of fruits and vegetables. Your children will soon start to reap the benefits of the vitamins, minerals, phytonutrients, and enzymes that these natural powerhouses contain.

FIVE REASONS TO HAVE FIVE A DAY

1 RAW ENERGY It is much better to consume most fruits and vegetables raw, because cooking destroys many of the vital enzymes that are fundamental to optimum health. A growing child relies on a diet rich in these enzymes in order to maintain a healthy metabolism, to digest and convert food into body tissue, and also to produce sufficient energy for the day ahead.

2 IMMUNE BOOSTER Eating plenty of colorful fruits and vegetables is like an insurance policy that guards against bugs and infections and helps prevent future degenerative diseases, because the phytonutrients that they contain detoxify the body, combat free radicals, and are essential for an effective immune system.

3 INSTANT HIT The nutrients in fruits and vegetables are usually released when the digestive process separates them from the indigestible fiber. Yet they are assimilated faster and in larger quantities when juiced.

4 REHYDRATION Fruits and vegetables contain a lot of water, a vital requirement of the human body because we are made up of about 60 percent H_2O ourselves. Those levels need constant replenishment, especially in active children. Soft drinks tend to dehydrate, so juices are a great choice.

5 ALL NATURAL Why would you even contemplate giving a child a drink that is full of dangerous additives, caffeine, and high levels of sugar or artificial sweeteners when the real thing tastes so much better and actually does them a power of good? A little effort now will be well worth it in the long run.

BECOME A RAINBOW WARRIOR

In order to make sure you are getting the best nutritional combination of vitamins, minerals, antioxidants, and phytochemicals, be sure that you eat red, green, yellow, orange, and purple fruits and vegetables. Get your children involved in picking out a colorful range of produce when you go shopping. Creating interest at this stage will help make them enthusiastic when it comes to actually making and drinking the juices and smoothies. You could even create a different color juice rota for each day of the week and get them to mark off when they have had their daily dose of green, yellow, red, purple, etc. Make it fun as well as healthy.

WHY BUY ORGANIC?

Long gone are the years where everything was grown in naturally fertilized soil and fruits and vegetables were eaten in season. The nutritional picture today is a different one:

• Fields are sprayed with herbicides, pesticides, and fungicides.

• Intensive farming methods are stripping the soil of vital minerals.

• Demand for out-of-season fruits and vegetables means they are being picked before they ripen, then transported and stored in refrigerated containers. By the time they reach supermarket shelves, the nutritional value has already been stripped.

• Organic produce is grown in sustainable farming conditions— no pesticides, artificial ingredients, preservatives, or irradiation.

If dealing with fruits and vegetables of unknown origin always:

• Remove skins of citrus fruits that may have been waxed.

• Peel nonorganic hard fruits and vegetables before juicing, or wash in warm water with a little dish-washing liquid, rinse thoroughly, and dry.

• Wash berries and leaves before using.

Utilize your freezer when organic produce, such as berries, melons, pineapples, bananas, grapes, and exotic fruit, including mangoes and papaya, are available. Simply wash berries, and peel and chop other fruit if necessary, then freeze on trays overnight and transfer to freezer containers or bags the next day. This ensures that the fruits are kept separate and are easy to remove instead of being fused in a large frozen lump.

HOW TO JUICE

The first step toward incorporating healthy juices and smoothies into your child's diet is to equip yourself with the proper appliances for the job.

Spend as much as you can afford on good-quality machines from a reputable manufacturer. Cheaper ones may seem a bargain, but all too often they break down after regular use. Experience tells that the cheaper the juicer, invariably the lower the quality of the resulting juice. A good-quality juicer will extract more of the nutrients held in the peel, pith, and seeds of certain fruits and vegetables so you can benefit from the full range of goodness they have to offer.

BLENDER

Look for a jug blender that has a variety of speeds because you will need to be able to crush ice and blend frozen fruit.

JUICERS

There are two main types of juicer. Whichever type you choose, a key point to note is that the drier the pulp, the more effective the juicer.

CENTRIFUGAL: This is the most widely used and affordable juicer.

Fruits and vegetables are fed into a rapidly spinning grater and the juice and pulp are separated.

MASTICATING: The larger, more expensive juicers are usually masticating or pulverizing. The fruits and vegetables are pushed through a wire mesh—this action is very powerful and produces a high level of juice with very dry pulp. Compared to the centrifugal juicer, the juice contains more nutrients because not only is there more of it, but it hasn't been extracted via a spinning metal blade, which produces heat that, in turn, kills those vital enzymes.

PULP ACTION

Instead of throwing away the fruit and vegetable pulp, it can be added to smoothies, muffins, soups, casseroles, meat dishes, etc., for added nutrition and fiber. If freezing, remember to add a little lemon juice.

JUICING HINTS

- Use fresh, firm fruits and vegetables for maximum nutrient content.
- Wash or scrub all fruits and vegetables thoroughly.
- Remove all stems and large pits.
- Pass fruits and vegetables through the juicer slowly and steadily using the pusher provided. Never use knives or other metal kitchen implements, and if your children are helping, make sure they are supervised.
- Do not cut fruits and vegetables too small; ideally, cut them to a size that fits comfortably into the chute.
- When juicing leafy vegetables, roll them into a ball and push through followed by harder fruit or vegetables, which will also help push through softer fruits.
- Don't try to juice bananas, avocados, or overripe fruit; they will clog the juicer. Use in smoothies instead.
- The most aggravating aspect of juicing is cleaning the machine after use; this has to be done immediately after you have finished juicing, and it has to be done thoroughly because any residue will harbor bacterial growth. For this reason, look for a machine that dismantles easily.
- Most machines come with a special brush to clean the mesh or grater. Wire cleaning pads are excellent for the job.

Homemade ice pops can be a healthy treat if made with natural fruit juice. Many of the recipes in this book are suitable for freezing.

JUICE YIELD

Juice yields will vary slightly according to the machine used and the ripeness and size of certain fruits, but, in general, the icons in this book represent the following volumes.

- 1 standard glass (about 1 cup)
- 1 small glass (about 2/3 cup)
- 1 ice lolly (about 1/3 cup)

The volume of ice pop molds depends on the brand. Because of this, allow for a slight variation in the number of ice pops each recipe makes.

TOP FRUITS AND VEGETABLES FOR JUICES AND SMOOTHIES

FRUITS

APPLES are a great juicing ingredient. They cleanse the digestive system and boost the immune system. They provide an excellent base for many juices, and even a small addition of apple will soften the taste of a stronger vegetable blend.

APRICOTS are a tasty addition to smoothies, either dried, fresh, or canned in their own juices. They are full of minerals and vitamins, especially vitamin A, immune boosting beta-carotene, and calcium. Apricots are also a good source of iron.

BANANAS are one of the classic smoothie staple ingredients, renowned for their energy-giving properties when you are busy and on the run, and for their ability to induce calm due to their high tryptophan content. They make a delicious ice cream substitute when pulped and frozen.

BLACK CURRANTS are hard to get, but if you grow your own or find them in a farmers' market, they are full of vitamin C. They mix well with apple and many children love their flavor.

BLUEBERRIES are a natural cure for diarrhea and will have a settling effect on upset stomachs. As with all berries, buy in bulk when they are in season and freeze.

CHERRIES contain powerful antioxidants. They don't have a high juice content, so they are better used in smoothies. They are a good source of folic acid, vitamin C, and calcium.

CRANBERRIES are both antiviral and antibiotic, but they are also sour, so they must be combined with sweeter fruit in juices and smoothies.

GRAPES, whether red or green, are intensely sweet and easy to juice and they will take the edge off slightly bitter vegetables. Their high glucose content makes them an effective boost for flagging children, and their high potassium levels make them ideal after exercise.

KIWIFRUITS are full of fiber and packed with vitamin C, which accelerates general healing and boosts the immune system.

PEACHES have a gentle laxative effect on the system and are good for calming irritated stomachs. Pureed peach with a little lemon and honey makes a great natural cough mixture.

PEARS Pear juice is fabulous if you are weaning a child because it rarely causes an allergic reaction. It is great for slow energy release and, when combined with prunes or peaches, it is an effective laxative.

MANGOES help boost the body's defenses because their high levels of vitamins A and C and beta-carotene prevent damage to cells by free radicals. They add fruity sweetness to citrus-base smoothies.

PINEAPPLES are anti-inflammatory, antiviral, and antibacterial and contain the digestive enzyme bromelain, which is essential in the digestion of protein. Avoid drinking pineapple juice by itself because it can damage tooth enamel.

MELONS are a highly nutritious ingredient. They are natural diuretics, powerful cleansers and detoxifiers. Because of their high water content, they are also great for rehydration.

RASPBERRIES contain natural aspirin and add great color to juices and smoothies. They can be slightly sharp, so combine with more mellow fruits to create child-friendly drinks that may help take the pain away.

ORANGES contain carotenoids, bioflavonoids, and loads of vitamin C. Citrus fruits are antiviral, antibacterial, and extremely versatile and flavorsome.

STRAWBERRIES will help keep your child from becoming anemic because they are high in vitamin C and folate, which is necessary for red blood cell manufacture. Whether in juices or smoothies, strawberries are a popular choice with children.

PAPAYA is great at aiding digestion because it contains the enzyme papain. This helps to break down protein. It also replenishes lost levels of vitamin C.

VEGETABLES

AVOCADOS are a complete food, packed with essential nutrients. Their high vitamin E content is excellent for maintaining a healthy skin, wound healing, and, of course, bolstering the immune system.

BEAN AND SEED SPROUTS

contain high levels of nutrients that are easy for the body to absorb. They are superfoods with a high protein, enzyme, vitamin, and mineral content. They protect against cancer and support every system in the body.

BEETS are high in folate, which is needed for red blood cell manufacture. It has a regulating effect on the digestive system, stimulating and strengthening the bowel, moving toxins out of the system. Kidney and liver function can be improved and the blood cleaned and fortified by regular consumption of beets, which are sweet and usually mixes well with many berries when juiced together.

BROCCOLI is a member of the cruciferous, or cabbage, family of vegetables. They are loaded with antioxidants and broccoli is pulsating with vitamin C. It is fantastic when mixed with sweet fruits, such as apple and pineapple.

CARROTS are nutrition powerhouses with a high beta-carotene content. They help to battle infections and boost your immunity. Carrots are effective against macular degeneration, too, and tend to blend well with other ingredients.

CELERY is a natural detoxifier and is great for cleansing the digestive system. It has a high potassium content so is great for rehydration.

CUCUMBER is a good base for many refreshing juices and smoothies. It is naturally diuretic and will stimulate the elimination of toxins through the urinary tract. Cucumber contains compounds, too, which are essential for healthy hair and skin nutrition.

LETTUCE contains high levels of folic acid, vitamin C, beta-carotene, and flavonols. Vary the type of lettuce you choose to juice because they all have slightly different phytonutrients. Essentially, they all have antioxidant properties, cleanse the digestive tract, and enhance the activity of bacteria in the digestive tract. It is a good choice to include in children's juices because it has a relatively mild taste.

SPINACH should be an integral part of the daily diet because, like all the leafy vegetables, it is rich in calcium, antioxidants, and beta-carotene. Mix spinach with sweeter fruit-base juices a couple of times every week for a great bone-building boost.

TOMATOES have got to be the best, most versatile ingredient known to humankind, and they are fantastic for our health. They lower the risk of cancer and heart disease because the presence of lycopene fights off free radicals. Although some children don't like them, they do mix well with most other fruits so can be disguised.

WHAT NOT TO JUICE

The following fruits and vegetables are not suitable for juicing:

EGGPLANTS—a member of the deadly nightshade family that should never be eaten raw because they contain a toxin called solanine, which may cause diarrhea, heart failure, headache, and vomiting in some sensitive people.

COCONUT—it will produce virtually no juice and almost definitely damage the juicer in the process.

LEEKS—simply don't juice well, but there is nothing wrong with eating young, tender ones raw.

RHUBARB—it contains high levels of kidney-damaging oxalic acid that is only removed by cooking.

Fruity Favorites

Strawberry sunrise

This deliciously refreshing juice has a high vitamin c content to ward off colds, so administer at the first sign of sniffles. strawberries are natural pain-killers and oranges are full of potassium, which is vital for rehydration, making this juice a good choice after tiring play. Freeze the liquid to make a great ice pop for sore throats.

Ingredients
• 8 ounces strawberries
• 2 oranges

1 Hull the strawberries.

2 Peel the oranges and divide the flesh into segments, then juice with the strawberries.

3 Serve straight over ice, or blend in a blender with a couple of ice cubes to make a cooling smoothie. Garnish with sliced strawberries, if desired.

GOOD SOURCE OF
VITAMIN C, POTASSIUM, AND CALCIUM

Fireball

··········· **MAKES** 2 standard glasses ···········

Packed with iron, calcium, and potassium, this all-around booster is great for bones and teeth. It is also really energizing, and when combined with a protein snack, such as nuts and seeds, it will keep busy kids on the go.

Ingredients
- 1 ripe mango
- ½ Galia or honeydew melon
- 1 cup orange juice

GOOD SOURCE OF
VITAMINS A AND C,
SELENIUM, AND ZINC

1 Peel the mango, remove the pit, and coarsely chop the flesh. Peel the melon, seed, and coarsely chop the flesh.

2 Put the mango and melon flesh into a blender.

3 Add the orange juice and a couple of ice cubes, then puree until smooth. Serve immediately.

Double C

A natural vitamin tonic that helps to support the immune system and keep bugs at bay. This makes a fantastic breakfast juice bolstered by the addition of kiwifruits, which contain even more vitamin c than oranges, so by combining the two fruits, you are giving your children an even more potent dose.

Ingredients
• 2 large oranges
• 3 kiwifruits, peeled, plus extra to garnish

1 Peel the oranges, leaving on as much pith as possible, and juice them along with the kiwifruits.

2 Serve over ice and garnish with a slice of kiwifruit, if desired.

GOOD SOURCE OF
VITAMINS A AND C, POTASSIUM, AND FOLIC ACID

Belly tickler

Apples are naturally cleansing, so they are great for a young digestive system that has overindulged in too much "party food." If you blend the juice in a blender with a couple of prunes, it can also alleviate constipation.

Ingredients
- 2 sweet crisp apples, such as Braeburn or Gala
- 1⅓ cups black currants or blueberries

GOOD SOURCE OF
VITAMIN C, CALCIUM, COPPER, ZINC, AND IRON

1 Juice the fruit and serve over ice for a great soft drink substitute.

2 Garnish with extra berries.

Sky high

This is the perfect juice for the young extreme sportsperson because it is high in energy-giving carbohydrates and, more importantly, the B vitamins needed to release that energy. Pineapple also helps digestion, due to the enzyme bromelain, which breaks down protein.

Ingredients

- ¼ fresh pineapple, or 1 (8-ounce) can pineapple chunks in its own juices
- 2 pears
- ½ lemon

GOOD SOURCE OF
VITAMINS B_1, B_6, AND C, CALCIUM, ZINC, AND COPPER

1 If using fresh pineapple, peel and cube the flesh.

2 Juice all the fruit and serve over ice.

Crazy kiwi

Weight for weight, kiwifruits contain more vitamin c than oranges. Making sure that there is enough of this vitamin in your child's diet is vital for general healing, because it plays a major role in most bodily functions.

Ingredients
- 2 ripe pears
- 3 kiwifruits

GOOD SOURCE OF
VITAMINS C AND B$_6$, COPPER, MAGNESIUM, PHOSPHORUS, AND CALCIUM

1 Wash the pears and peel the kiwifruits.

2 Slice the fruit into even pieces, then juice.

3 Pour the juice into a glass, add a couple of ice cubes, if desired, and garnish with slices of kiwifruit, if desired.

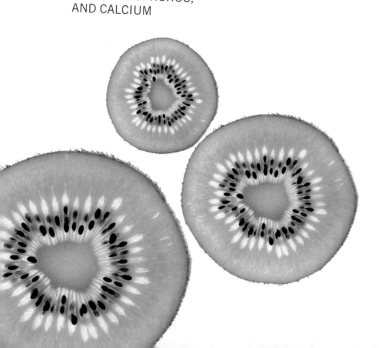

GOOD SOURCE OF
VITAMINS C, B₁, AND B₂, NIACIN, B₆,
FOLIC ACID, COPPER, POTASSIUM,
CALCIUM, MAGNESIUM,
AND PHOSPHORUS

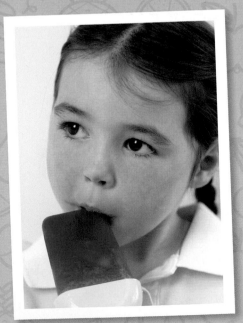

Berry bouncer

An excellent summertime refresher, especially when
the sun-ripened berries are at their most plentiful.
Buy extra and freeze so you can inject a little
sunshine all year round. The calcium and iron
content helps to prevent fatigue. Makes
a good ice pop for sore throats.

Ingredients

- 4 ounces strawberries
  (about 1 cup prepared)
- ½ cup red currants
  or blueberries
- ½ orange
- ½ cup water
- ½ teaspoon honey (optional)

1 Hull the strawberries, remove the spigs
from the red currants, and peel the orange.

2 Juice the fruit and add the water. Stir in
the honey, if using.

3 Pour into pop molds and freeze.

4 If serving as a drink, add ice cubes, if
desired, and garnish with red currants
or blueberries, if desired.

Energy bubble

This juice is high in natural carbohydrates, which are essential for growing children. It is especially good before exercise because it is a great energy provider. Because the mango is full of sweetness, you can use fairly tart varieties of apple.

Ingredients
- 3 apples, preferably red
- 2 passion fruits
- 1 mango

GOOD SOURCE OF
VITAMINS A AND C,
POTASSIUM, MAGNESIUM,
PHOSPHORUS, AND IRON

1 Wash the apples and chop them into even pieces.

2 Slice the passion fruits in half, scoop out the flesh, and discard the seeds.

3 Peel the mango and remove the pit. Juice all the ingredients.

4 Pour the juice into glasses and add some ice cubes.

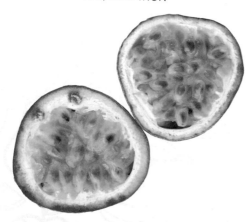

Go green

High carb, mineral rich, and a beautifully sweet energizing fuel for kids on the go, this is perfect for sports fans and busy little bees. Tart apples, such as Granny Smiths, provide a good counterbalance to the melon and pineapple, and the high water content of the melons makes this juice refreshing.

Ingredients
- ½ Galia or honeydew melon
- ¼ pineapple
- 3 green apples

1 Remove the skin and deseed the melon.

2 Remove the skin and hard core from the pineapple.

3 Chop all the fruit into even pieces and juice.

4 Pour into a glass and add a couple of ice cubes.

GOOD SOURCE OF
VITAMINS C, B_1, B_2, AND B_6,
COPPER, POTASSIUM,
MAGNESIUM, PHOSPHORUS,
AND CALCIUM

Yellow submarine

This is a good drink to have with a lunch because the bromelain helps to break down protein, and the B vitamins are necessary to release energy from carbohydrates. It will keep kids going for hours.

Ingredients

- ¼ pineapple
- 2 pears

GOOD SOURCE OF
VITAMINS C, B_1, AND B_6,
CALCIUM, IRON, AND COPPER

1 Peel the pineapple and remove the core.

2 Chop all the fruit into even pieces and juice it.

3 Pour into a glass and add a couple of ice cubes.

Plum yummy

If you choose plums that are ripe but not overripe, you will find it easier to remove the pits before juicing. Plums contain potassium and iron and have laxative properties, and this juice will guarantee your child gets more than the recommended apple a day.

Ingredients
- 5 ripe plums
- 3 red apples

GOOD SOURCE OF
VITAMINS A, C, AND B_6,
NIACIN, COPPER,
IRON, AND POTASSIUM

1 Slice the plums into quarters and remove the pits.

2 Cut the apples into even pieces.

3 Juice the fruit and serve in a glass over a couple of ice cubes.

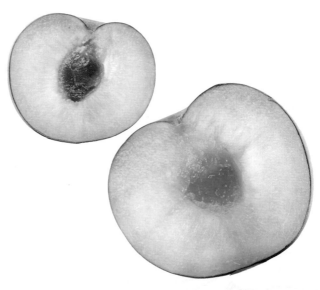

Golden wonder

MAKES 2 standard glasses

The wonder of this golden nectar is how full of beta-carotene, vitamin c, and iron it is. The vitamin c helps the absorption of the iron, which makes it an ideal choice for any child feeling a little below par.

Ingredients
- 3 apricots
- 1 large nectarine or peach
- 2 passion fruits
- ⅔ cup fresh apple juice

1 Cut the apricots in half and discard the pits.

2 Cut the nectarine or peach in half and discard the pit. (If your children prefer smooth drinks, peel the fruit before you start.)

3 Cut the passion fruits in half, scoop out the pulp, and push through a strainer to remove the seeds.

4 Put everything into a blender with a couple of ice cubes and blend until smooth.

GOOD SOURCE OF
VITAMINS A AND C, IRON,
BETA-CAROTENE,
AND POTASSIUM

Battery charge

······· **MAKES** 1 standard glass ············

This juice will help get your child through the day because it contains large amounts of carbohydrate for energy release, plus a hefty amount of vitamin c, which helps to increase oxygen uptake and energy production. Try combining it with a protein snack, such as cheese, to regulate blood sugar and maintain consistent performance.

Ingredients
- 2 kiwifruits
- 2 cups seedless green grapes

1 Peel the kiwifruits and juice them with the grapes.

2 Pour the juice into a glass and add a couple of ice cubes.

3 Garnish with kiwifruit slices, if desired.

GOOD SOURCE OF
VITAMINS C, B_1, AND B_6, COPPER, POTASSIUM, MAGNESIUM, PHOSPHORUS, AND CALCIUM

Jump-start

This is a good juice to drink during sports activities because it is isotonic—it replenishes potassium levels and quenches thirst. Grapes are a good source of glucose and fructose and are the perfect energy snack.

Ingredients

- ⅛ small Galia or honeydew melon
- ½ cup seedless green grapes
- ⅔ cup water

1 Peel the melon and seed the flesh.

2 Juice the melon and grapes.

3 Add the water, pour into glasses, then add ice cubes.

GOOD SOURCE OF
VITAMINS A, C, B$_1$, AND B$_6$, MAGNESIUM, PHOSPHORUS COPPER, AND POTASSIUM

Red devil

A high water content and high glycemic value makes this a perfect juice to drink before exercise. As well as copious amounts of vitamin c, it provides potassium, which is vital for muscle and nerve function and might relieve tired legs.

Ingredients
- ¼ watermelon (about 2 cups prepared)
- 1 cup raspberries

1 Remove the skin and seed the watermelon.

2 Chop the flesh into pieces.

3 Juice all the fruit, pour into a glass, and add some crushed ice cubes, if desired.

GOOD SOURCE OF
VITAMINS C AND B$_6$,
FOLIC ACID, CALCIUM, COPPER, AND POTASSIUM

Sweet and sour

cranberries may not seem an obvious choice for children because of their sourness, but they are so rich in vitamin c that it is worth including them in juices and smoothies. This juice combines the sweetness of the mango and orange with a spoonful of honey that counteracts the sharpness of the berries and rev up the vitamin c content even more. When fresh cranberries are not in season, use frozen ones instead, but defrost them first.

Ingredients

- 1 mango
- 1 orange
- 1¼ cups cranberries
- ½ cup water
- 1 teaspoon honey

1 Peel the mango and remove the pit.

2 Peel the orange and divide the flesh into segments.

3 Juice all the fruits, pour the juice into a glass, and stir in the water and honey.

4 Add a couple of ice cubes, if desired, and drink immediately.

GOOD SOURCE OF
VITAMINS A, C, B_1, AND B_6, COPPER, POTASSIUM, CALCIUM, AND IRON

Frisky frog

A sweet juice full of carbohydrates and calcium, this is perfect for revving up flagging energy levels. Try serving it with a nutty snack bar or a handful of almonds and your child will soon be revived and leaping around.

- 2 kiwifruits
- ⅓ small honeydew melon
- 1 cup seedless green grapes

1 Put one peeled kiwifruit into a blender and process until smooth.

2 Spoon into the bottom of the pop molds and freeze until set.

3 Remove the skin and seeds from the melon. Peel the second kiwifruit. Chop the melon and kiwifruits into even pieces.

4 Juice all the fruits, then pour the juice into the already-frozen pop molds and freeze until solid.

GOOD SOURCE OF
VITAMINS C, B_6, AND B_1,
COPPER, POTASSIUM,
MAGNESIUM, PHOSPHORUS,
AND CALCIUM

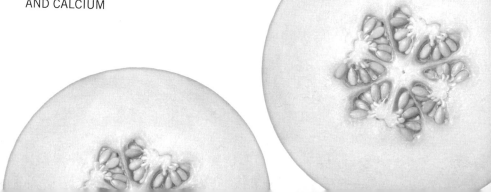

Princess peachy

This cooling juice supplies almost a complete daily quota of beta-carotene. This is converted by the body into vitamin A, which is vital for healthy growth and development.

Ingredients
- 3 apricots
- 1 peach
- 2 apples

GOOD SOURCE OF
VITAMINS A AND C,
MAGNESIUM, IRON, AND ZINC

1 Halve and pit the apricots and peach.

2 Juice the apples, apricots, and peach.

3 Pour the juice into a blender with a few ice cubes and blend for 10 seconds. Serve in a tall glass.

Apple aid

Apple and blackberry are a classic combination, but blackberries can be tart, so it is best to choose a sweet variety of apple, such as Braeburn, Pink Lady, Pippin, or Golden Delicious. Blackberries are a good source of vitamin E, which is necessary for healing both inside and out, making this juice a liquid band aid for all those cuts and grazes.

Ingredients
- 3 apples
- ⅔ cup blackberries
- 1¼ cups water

1 Slice the apples into even pieces. Juice the fruits, then stir in the water.

2 Serve over ice cubes.

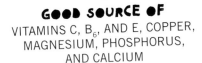

GOOD SOURCE OF
VITAMINS C, B_6, AND E, COPPER, MAGNESIUM, PHOSPHORUS, AND CALCIUM

Time out

Melons are full of carotenoids and blackberries are a great source of anthocyanidins. Your children might not be able spell these powerful phytonutrients, but rest assured that this antioxidant punch will put the color back in their cheeks.

Ingredients
- ⅔ cup cubed cantaloupe
- ⅔ cup fresh or frozen blackberries
- 2 kiwifruits
- ½ cup apple juice

1 Juice the melon, blackberries, and kiwifruits (no need to peel them), then put them into a blender with the apple juice and process with a couple of ice cubes.

2 Pour into a glass and serve. Garnish with a few blackberries.

GOOD SOURCE OF
VITAMINS A AND C AND MAGNESIUM

Berry cherry sparklers

·········· **MAKES** 3 standard glasses ··········

When the temperature is soaring, prepare this great summer cocktail, bursting with vitamin c. It is a perfect treat for a group of hot and sweaty kids.

Ingredients

- 4 ounces strawberries (about 1 cup prepared)
- 1 cup fresh cherries
- 1 slice watermelon (1 cup small chunks)
- ½ cup orange juice
- 2 cups sparkling water, chilled

1 Hull the strawberries.

2 Halve and pit the cherries.

3 Seed the watermelon and cut it into small chunks.

4 Put all the fruit into a blender with the orange juice and blend until smooth. If your child prefers a smooth drink, strain the fruit puree over a bowl to remove the skin and seeds.

5 Pour the puree into the glasses. Top up with the sparkling water.

GOOD SOURCE OF
VITAMIN C, CALCIUM, MAGNESIUM, POTASSIUM, AND BETA-CAROTENE

Hug in a glass

MAKES 1 standard glass

If your child is under the weather and can't face food, maybe this simple juice will hit the spot and help him or her on the road to recovery. The addition of honey gives a much needed energy boost, and the vitamin c content will help a struggling immune system.

Ingredients
- 2 oranges
- 1 red apple
- 1 pear
- 1 teaspoon honey (optional)

GOOD SOURCE OF
VITAMINS C, B$_1$, B$_2$, AND B$_6$, FOLIC ACID, CALCIUM, COPPER, POTASSIUM, MAGNESIUM, AND PHOSPHORUS

1 Peel the oranges and divide the flesh into segments.

2 Chop the apple and pear into even pieces.

3 Juice all the fruits and pour into a glass.

4 Stir in the honey, if using, and add a couple of ice cubes, if desired.

Raspberry crush

····· **MAKES** 4 small glasses ·····

With isotonic juices like this, you can confidently throw away commercial soft drinks that are high in additives and sugar. Refreshing, revitalizing, and full of vitamin C, this will sustain—not drain—your child.

Ingredients
- 2 large oranges
- 1½ cups raspberries
- 1 cup water

1 Peel the oranges and divide the flesh into segments.

2 Juice all the fruits, then add the water.

3 Pour the juice into glasses and add a couple of ice cubes, if desired.

GOOD SOURCE OF
VITAMINS C, B_6, AND B_1, FOLATE, ZINC, COPPER, CALCIUM, IRON, AND POTASSIUM

Iron kid

Iron deficiency in children is a nutritional problem worldwide. This juice provides useful amounts of this important mineral, which helps transport oxygen around the body, and aids overall performance both in the classroom and on the sports field.

••

Ingredients
- 2 peaches
- 1¼ cups water
- 1 red apple
- 4 ounces strawberries
  (about 1 cup prepared)

1 Remove the pits from the peaches, chop the flesh into even chunks, and juice.

2 Add one-third of the water and divide evenly among the pop molds. Freeze until just set.

3 Chop the apples into even chunks and juice. Add one-third of the water, pour on top of the frozen peach mixture, then freeze until just set.

4 Hull the strawberries, then juice them. Add the remainder of the water, pour on top of the frozen apple mixture, then freeze until set.

GOOD SOURCE OF
VITAMIN C, COPPER,
POTASSIUM, MAGNESIUM,
PHOSPHORUS, AND IRON

Doctor, doctor

This juice packs a mighty antiviral punch because it is full of vitamin C. Dispense at regular intervals along with the chicken soup and hugs when your child is a little under the weather. One juice daily will help to keep those bugs and viruses away.

Ingredients
- 2 oranges
- 1 kiwifruit, peeled
- 8 ounces strawberries

GOOD SOURCE OF
VITAMIN C, POTASSIUM, MAGNESIUM, AND CALCIUM

1 Peel the oranges and divide the flesh into several segments.

2 Coarsely chop the kiwifruit, setting aside a piece for decoration.

3 Hull the strawberries. Juice the fruit.

4 Serve in a tall glass with ice and a chunk of kiwifruit.

Run rabbit run

AS well as being a vitamin-enriched tonic, this juice is an excellent natural laxative. For added potency, stir in a couple of tablespoons of prune juice and serve with a handful of pumpkin seeds to nibble on.

Ingredients
- 2 pears
- 2 apples

GOOD SOURCE OF
VITAMIN C, POTASSIUM, MAGNESIUM, AND PECTIN

1 Coarsely chop the pears and apples, including the cores.

2 Juice the apples and pears, then blend in a blender with a couple of ice cubes.

3 Pour into a tall glass and serve.

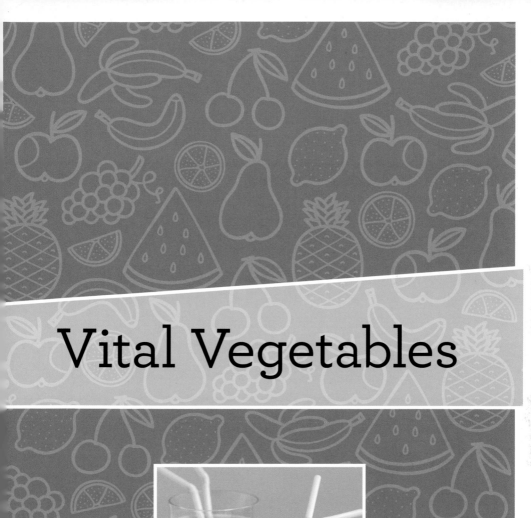

Vital Vegetables

Captain Zinger

MAKES 1 standard glass

If your child likes a touch of spice, add a little fresh ginger to this tasty combination, which benefits the immune system, supports good eyesight, and provides selenium and zinc for a brain power boost.

Ingredients
- ¼ cantaloupe
- 1 lime
- 2 carrots
- ½-inch piece fresh ginger

1 Peel, seed, and cube the melon.

2 Peel the lime.

3 Juice the carrots, melon, lime, and ginger.

4 Serve in a glass, over ice, if desired.

GOOD SOURCE OF
VITAMINS A AND C,
SELENIUM, AND ZINC

Green dream

Sprouts are newly germinated seeds and beans. These baby plants are full of the nutrition needed to produce a fully grown plant—anti-oxidants, vitamins, minerals, and trace elements—ideal for a growing child.

Ingredients

- 3 celery sticks
- 2 tart apples, such as Granny Smith
- ⅔ cup alfalfa sprouts

GOOD SOURCE OF
VITAMINS A, C, B$_6$, AND K, POTASSIUM, FOLIC ACID, IRON, AND CALCIUM

1 Cut the celery and the apples into even-sized pieces.

2 Rinse the alfalfa.

3 Feed all the ingredients into a juicer in alternating batches.

4 Pour into a glass, add a couple of ice cubes, and drink immediately.

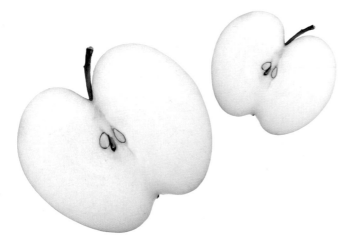

Power pack

Juices give instant energy, so they are fabulous when little ones are getting a little lethargic. Turn off the television, give them a juice, and send them out for some fresh air. It will put color back on their cheeks.

Ingredients

- 4 ounces strawberries (about 1 cup prepared)
- 4 carrots
- 2 small beets
- 1 orange

1 Hull the strawberries.

2 Juice the carrots, beets, and orange and blend in a blender with the strawberries and a few ice cubes.

3 Garnish with a strawberry.

GOOD SOURCE OF VITAMINS A AND C, POTASSIUM, MAGNESIUM, AND SELENIUM

Juice boost

This juice is sweet enough for a child to enjoy,
especially with the addition of orange. Perhaps prepare
it as an appetizer before a meal, or serve with lunch—
a godsend for kids who won't eat vegetables.

Ingredients

- 4 tomatoes
- 2 oranges, peeled
- 2 celery sticks, plus leafy tops
- 2 carrots

1 Juice all the ingredients, except for the leafy tops.

2 Pour the juice over ice cubes in glasses and serve with leafy celery top stirrers.

GOOD SOURCE OF
VITAMIN C, BETA-CAROTENE,
POTASSIUM, LYCOPENE,
FOLATE, AND SODIUM

Magic juice

This is a great juice for children to help you make, because they can cast a spell as they clean and chop— carrots to help you to see, an orange to scare away colds, and an apple a day to keep the doctor away.

Ingredients
- 3 carrots
- 1 orange
- 1 tart apple, such as Granny Smith

1 Scrub the carrots. Peel the orange and divide into segments.

2 Cut the carrots and apple into even pieces.

3 Juice all of the ingredients, pour the juice into a glass, then add a few ice cubes, if desired.

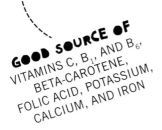

GOOD SOURCE OF VITAMINS C, B₁, AND B₆, BETA-CAROTENE, FOLIC ACID, POTASSIUM, CALCIUM, AND IRON

Orange refresher

Papaya helps to calm the digestive system, cucumber flushes out toxins, and orange gives a great boost of vitamin c. The overall effect is calming and rehydrating, so all you have to do is take one hot, sweaty, overtired child, add one glass of Orange Refresher, then sit back and relax.

Ingredients
- ½ small papaya
- ½ cucumber
- 2 oranges

GOOD SOURCE OF
VITAMINS A AND C,
MAGNESIUM, POTASSIUM,
AND SELENIUM

1 Peel the papaya, cucumber, and the oranges (leaving on as much of the pith as possible).

2 Juice them together and serve in a tall glass over ice. Garnish with slices of cucumber and papaya, if desired.

Cool juice

This naturally sweet juice is great if your child has been overdoing it and feels below par. Strawberries are a good source of vitamin c and have antiviral and antibiotic properties, while melon and cucumber both rehydrate and cleanse the system, which is essential for healthy liver, kidneys, and adrenal glands.

Ingredients

- 4 ounces strawberries (about 1 cup prepared)
- ½ cup Galia or honeydew melon chunks
- ¼ cucumber

1 Hull the strawberries, then juice with the melon and cucumber.

2 Serve over ice in a tall glass, garnished with cucumber slices, if desired.

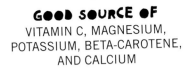

GOOD SOURCE OF
VITAMIN C, MAGNESIUM, POTASSIUM, BETA-CAROTENE, AND CALCIUM

Easy rider

If your child is prone to travel sickness, the ginger in this juice will help to alleviate nausea. It also aids digestion and wards off colds — an all-around winner really.

Ingredients
- 2 carrots
- 1 tart apple, such as Granny Smith
- ½-inch piece fresh ginger

1 Cut the carrots, apple, and ginger into even pieces and juice.

2 Pour into a glass and add a couple of ice cubes.

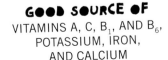

GOOD SOURCE OF
VITAMINS A, C, B$_1$, AND B$_6$,
POTASSIUM, IRON,
AND CALCIUM

Wacky wizard

MAKES 1 standard glass

Juicing is a good way to gradually introduce vegetables into the diets of fussy children, especially when they are combined with sweet fruits. Cucumber is extremely hydrating, making this a great cooling drink for active kids.

Ingredients
- ½ mango
- 2 apples, peeled
- ½ cucumber, peeled

1 Juice the ingredients.

2 Blend with a couple of ice cubes to get a fruity slush.

GOOD SOURCE OF
VITAMINS A AND C, CALCIUM, AND POTASSIUM

Maybe baby

Technically, it is a fruit, but many people classify the nutrient-dense avocado as a vegetable. Whatever its official status, it does make a fantastically complete baby food, especially when combined with gentle pears. If you want to turn this into a tasty smoothie, triple the amount of pear you juice, then blend in a blender with a little ice.

Ingredients
- ½ small avocado
- 1 small pear

1 Peel the avocado and remove the pit.

2 Juice the pear and blend with the avocado.

GOOD SOURCE OF
VITAMINS C, B, AND E, POTASSIUM, AND MAGNESIUM

Wake-up time

Perfect for children who love milk but it doesn't love them—a sweet dairy-free treat that will nourish and sustain your child but will not send their blood sugar levels rocketing into orbit.

Ingredients

- ¼ pineapple
- 1 parsnip
- 2 small carrots
- ⅓ cup soy milk

GOOD SOURCE OF
VITAMIN C, POTASSIUM,
BETA-CAROTENE, CALCIUM,
AND FOLATE

1 Peel the pineapple, remove the core, and cut the flesh into chunks.

2 Juice the pineapple, parsnip, and carrots. Blend in a blender with the soy milk and a couple of ice cubes.

3 Garnish with pineapple wedges, if desired.

Glow in the dark

Full of iron, calcium, and potassium, this nondairy smoothie is great for bones and teeth and keeping colds at bay. Bananas are also packed with tryptophan, which is renowned for its calming properties, so this is a good one to have at the end of a busy day.

Ingredients
- 2 large carrots
- 1 small orange
- 1 small banana
- 6 dried apricots

1 Juice the carrots and orange.

2 Blend in a blender with the banana, apricots, and some ice cubes.

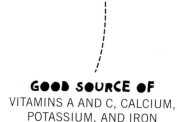

GOOD SOURCE OF
VITAMINS A AND C, CALCIUM, POTASSIUM, AND IRON

Green grass

An ultragreen juice with a sweet flavor and
a powerful vitamin punch that will help maintain
energy levels and maybe tempt someone who
just won't eat their greens.

Ingredients

- ⅓ bunch of broccoli
- 2 sweet, crisp apples, such as Braeburn or Cox
- 2 cups spinach
- ⅓ cup green grapes

1 Coarsely chop the broccoli and quarter the apples.

2 Juice everything, then blend in a blender with a few ice cubes.

GOOD SOURCE OF
VITAMINS A AND C,
SELENIUM, AND ZINC

Supersmoothies

Superstripy

Sometimes it's all about the presentation—and this smoothie is well worth the effort. Tasty and bursting with nutrients, it makes a wonderful breakfast treat.

Ingredients

- 2 cups raspberries
- 1 cup apple juice
- 1⅓ cups blueberries
- ¼ cup Greek yogurt
- ½ cup skimd milk
- 1 tablespoon honey, or to taste
- 1 tablespoon wheat germ (optional)

1 Puree the raspberries with half of the apple juice.

2 Puree the blueberries with the remaining apple juice.

3 Mix together the yogurt, milk, honey, and wheat germ, if using. Add a spoonful of the raspberry puree.

4 Pour the blueberry puree into the glass. Carefully pour the yogurt mixture on top and, finally, pour the raspberry puree over the surface of the yogurt. Serve chilled.

GOOD SOURCE OF
VITAMIN C, CALCIUM, IRON, MAGNESIUM, POTASSIUM, PHOSPHORUS, AND ZINC

Nutty professor

Unless your child is allergic to nuts, this fabulously creamy smoothie will make a fantastic snack that keeps hunger pangs at bay and is so much better than a couple of cookies or package of potato chips. If your child is lactose intolerant, you can use rice or soy milk.

Ingredients
- 1 ripe banana
- 1¼ cups low-fat milk
- 1 tablespoon smooth peanut butter

1 Peel and slice the banana, put it in a freezer container, and freeze for at least 2 hours or overnight.

2 Put the banana, milk, and peanut butter into a blender and blend until smooth. Serve immediately.

GOOD SOURCE OF
VITAMINS C, B₁, B₂, B₆, AND B₁₂, FOLIC ACID, NIACIN, CALCIUM, COPPER, POTASSIUM, ZINC, MAGNESIUM, AND PHOSPHORUS

Starburst

This high-carbohydrate, low-fat smoothie is a great choice for refueling and soothing tired muscles. Bananas are high in potassium, a vital mineral for muscle and nerve function. This is great for breakfast or as a midafternoon snack with a granola bar or some rice cakes and hummus.

Ingredients

- 1 small, ripe banana
- 3 ouces strawberries (about ¾ cup prepared)
- 1 cup orange juice

GOOD SOURCE OF
VITAMINS C, B_1, AND B_6, FOLIC ACID, MAGNESIUM, ZINC, AND PHOSPHORUS

1 Peel the banana and hull the strawberries. Put the fruits into a freezer container and freeze for at least 2 hours or overnight.

2 Put the frozen fruits and the juice into a blender and blend until thick. Garnish with a few strawberries, if desired, and serve immediately.

Pink princess

MAKES 2 small glasses

Ripe berries are packed with vitamins B and C.
They have a deep color and rich flavor and so are
ideal for making smoothies. Nutritionally, frozen fruits
are every bit as good as fresh, and they are available all
year round. Soy milk is a good alternative to cow milk
for children who are lactose intolerant, but look for
a calcium-enriched brand for maximum nutrition.

Ingredients

- 1 cup frozen mixed berries, such as raspberries, blueberries, and hulled strawberries
- 1¼ cups vanilla-flavor soy milk
- 1 teaspoon honey (optional)

1 Put the berries, soy milk, and honey, if using, into a blender and blend until thick.

2 Serve immediately, garnished with extra berries, if desired.

GOOD SOURCE OF
VITAMINS C, B_1, B_2, AND B_6, FOLIC
ACID, COPPER, POTASSIUM, ZINC,
MAGNESIUM, PHOSPHORUS,
CALCIUM, AND IRON

Purple tiger

This smoothie is so thick you might need a spoon to eat it, making it a fantastic summer dessert. Try layering the mango and berries in an ice-pop container to make a cooling burst of fruity goodness that children will love.

Ingredients

- 3 mangoes
- 2 tablespoons mango sorbet
- ½ cup apple juice
- 1⅓ cups black currants or blueberries

GOOD SOURCE OF
VITAMIN C, BETA-CAROTENE, POTASSIUM, MAGNESIUM, ZINC, AND CALCIUM

1 Peel the mangoes and remove their pits, then cube the flesh.

2 Puree the mango with the mango sorbet and half the apple juice. Set aside to chill.

3 Puree the berries with the rest of the juice.

4 To serve, divide the smoothie between two glasses.

5 Place a spoon on the surface of the mango, holding it as flat as you can, and pour the berry puree over the top.

6 Drag a teaspoon or toothpick down the inside of the glass to make vertical stripes around the glass.

Tutti-frutti

Juices and smoothies are wonderful for keeping energy levels high when little ones won't eat. Instead of sitting a child formally at a dinner table, why not place a glass of this delicious juice within easy reach, along with a few high-protein snacks, and let them graze for a change—remember battles about food are invariably about pushing boundaries and power struggles.

Ingredients

- 1 mango
- 3 apples, preferably red ones
- 2 passion fruits

GOOD SOURCE OF
VITAMINS A AND C,
POTASSIUM, MAGNESIUM,
PHOSPHORUS, AND IRON

1 Peel the mango and remove the pit. Cut the mango and apples into even pieces.

2 Slice the passion fruits in half, scoop out the flesh, and discard the seeds. Juice all the ingredients.

3 Pour the juice into a glass and add a couple of ice cubes, if desired.

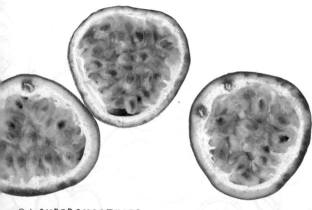

Traffic light

A colorful thick smoothie that is an excellent source of many nutrients. You can vary the fruits you use— just be sure to stick to the red/yellow/green format if you want it to be a true traffic light.

Ingredients

- 3 kiwifruits
- ⅔ cup tangy flavored yogurt, such as lemon or orange
- 1 small mango
- 2 tablespoons orange or apple juice
- 1 cup raspberries
- 1–2 teaspoons honey

GOOD SOURCE OF
VITAMIN C, BETA-CAROTENE,
POTASSIUM, CALCIUM,
AND MAGNESIUM

1 Peel and coarsely chop the kiwifruits, then blend in a blender until smooth.

2 Spoon the kiwi mixture into two tall glasses. Top each glass with a spoonful of yogurt, spreading the yogurt all the way to the sides of the glasses.

3 Peel the mango, remove the pit, and chop the flesh coarsely. Blend the mango to a puree with the orange or apple juice and spoon into the glasses. Top with another layer of yogurt.

4 Blend the raspberries and push through a strainer over a bowl to extract the seeds. Check their sweetness. You might need to stir in a little honey if they're sharp.

5 Spoon the raspberry puree into the glasses.

Black beauty

A delicious smoothie that provides calcium to
support growing teeth and bones. If your child is
lactose intolerant or regularly has colds and sinus
problems, use soy yogurt. You can also substitute
strawberries or raspberries.

Ingredients
- 1⅓ cups black currants, blackberries, or blueberries
- ½ cup apple juice
- 1¼ cups plain yogurt
- 2 tablespoons honey

1 If using black currants, remove any stray "spigs." Reserve a few pieces of fruit for decoration, then freeze the remainder for 2 hours or overnight.

2 Blend the frozen berries in a blender with the apple juice and half the yogurt until combined.

3 Spoon into glasses. Combine the rest of the yogurt with the honey.

4 Spoon the yogurt over the fruit mixture and serve garnished with a few berries.

GOOD SOURCE OF
VITAMIN C, CALCIUM,
AND MAGNESIUM

Apricot cloud

This smoothie is an excellent source of calcium, providing almost one-third of the daily requirement. calcium is essential for helping to build and maintain good bone health, and it is also involved in nerve transmission, blood clotting, and muscle function. canned apricots in natural juice are a handy pantry standby and provide an extra source of carbohydrate.

Ingredients

- ½ (15-ounce) can apricots in natural juice, drained
- ⅔ cup apricot yogurt
- ⅔ cup ice-cold, low-fat milk

1 Put the apricots, yogurt, and milk into a blender and blend until smooth.

2 Pour into glasses and garnish with slices of apricot, if desired. Drink immediately.

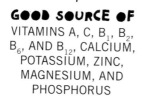

GOOD SOURCE OF
VITAMINS A, C, B_1, B_2, B_6, AND B_{12}, CALCIUM, POTASSIUM, ZINC, MAGNESIUM, AND PHOSPHORUS

Orange blossom

Orange juice is abundant in vitamin c, which is vital for the absorption of iron in the body—a good choice if your child is anemic or recovering from an illness.

Ingredients

- 4 ounces strawberries (about 1 cup prepared)
- 1 small ripe mango
- 1¼ cups orange juice or 3 oranges, juiced

GOOD SOURCE OF
VITAMINS A, C, B_1, B_2, AND B_6, FOLIC ACID, COPPER, POTASSIUM, MAGNESIUM, PHOSPHORUS, CALCIUM, AND IRON

1 Hull the strawberries and freeze for 2 hours or overnight.

2 Peel the mango, remove the pit, and chop the flesh coarsely.

3 Put the strawberries, mango, and orange juice into a blender and blend until smooth.

4 Pour into pop molds and freeze until set.

Milky mango

Bananas are a perfect base for a creamy smoothie and wonderful for active children because they are rich in carbohydrate and potassium. They also contain a special fiber—fructoligosaccharides—which encourages the growth of healthy bacteria in the stomach.

- 1 ripe banana
- 1 ripe mango
- 1 cup orange juice
- 1 cup low-fat milk
- 3 tablespoons fromage blanc or Greek yogurt

GOOD SOURCE OF
VITAMINS A, C, B$_1$, B$_2$, B$_6$, AND B$_{12}$, FOLIC ACID, CALCIUM, POTASSIUM, MAGNESIUM, AND PHOSPHORUS

1 Peel and slice the banana. Peel the mango, remove the pit, and coarsely chop the flesh.

2 Put the banana, mango, orange juice, milk, fromage blanc or yogurt, and a couple of ice cubes into a blender and blend until smooth.

3 Pour into glasses and serve immediately.

Big purple monster

Blackberries and purple grape juice contain antioxidants that are excellent for general health. Purple grape juice is also a good source of potassium, which is essential for optimum nerve, cell, and muscle function. Adding quark or fromage blanc gives this drink a creamy taste and texture, and also boosts the calcium and protein content. If you cannot find quark or fromage frais, use Greek or regular plain yogurt instead.

Ingredients
- 1 cup frozen blackberries
- 1¼ cups purple grape juice
- 3 tablespoons quark or fromage blanc
- 1 teaspoon honey (optional)

1 Put the berries, juice, and quark or fromage blanc into a blender, add the honey, if using.

2 Blend until thick.

GOOD SOURCE OF
VITAMINS C, B_1, B_2, B_6, AND B_{12}, FOLIC ACID, CALCIUM, IRON, MAGNESIUM, PHOSPHORUS, AND POTASSIUM

Jumping jack

········· **MAKES** 2 small glasses ·········

The combination of bananas, ground almonds, and soy milk makes this a highly nutritious drink. It is best to use very ripe bananas (really yellow skin with black spots). Almonds are an excellent source of vitamin E as well as many minerals.

Ingredients

- 1 very ripe banana
- 1 cup soy milk
- 3 tablespoons ground almonds (almond meal)
- pinch of ground cinnamon
- a little honey (optional)

GOOD SOURCE OF

VITAMINS C, E, B_1, B_2, AND B_6, NIACIN, FOLIC ACID, COPPER, POTASSIUM, ZINC, MAGNESIUM, PHOSPHORUS, AND CALCIUM

1 Peel and slice the banana, put it into a freezer container, and freeze for at least 2 hours or overnight.

2 Put the frozen banana, soy milk, ground almonds, and cinnamon into a blender, add the honey, if using, and blend until thick and frothy.

3 Pour into a glass and serve immediately with ice cubes and garnished with ground cinnamon.

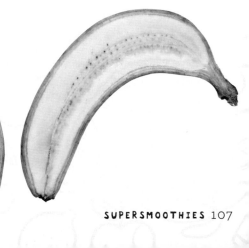

Peachy orange blend

······· **MAKES** 2 standard glasses ·········

No time to prepare fruit? Don't worry—this is a quick, simple-to-make healthy smoothie that can be ready in a minute. Perfect for busy moms and independent kids who want to help in the kitchen, it's high in calcium and immune-boosting beta-carotenes.

Ingredients
- 1 (15-ounce) can peaches in natural juice, drained
- ⅔ cup peach or apricot yogurt
- 1 cup orange juice
- a little honey (optional)

1 Put the peaches into a blender with the yogurt, orange juice, and honey, if using, and blend until smooth.

2 Add a couple of ice cubes, if desired, and top with a swirl of any remaining yogurt.

GOOD SOURCE OF
VITAMINS C, B₁, B₂ AND B₆, FOLIC ACID, CALCIUM, POTASSIUM AND PHOSPHORUS

Little pinky

This is a deliciously sweet, yet refreshing drink and great for rehydration after sports and exercise, when energy reserves are used up. If you cannot find passion fruit juice, try using pineapple juice instead.

Ingredients

- ¼ watermelon
  (about 2 cups prepared)
- 2 kiwifruits
- 1 cup passion fruit juice

1 Peel and seed the watermelon and dice the flesh.

2 Put it into a freezer container and freeze for at least 2 hours or overnight.

3 Peel and coarsely chop the kiwifruits, then put them into a blender with the melon and passion fruit juice and process until thick. Serve immediately.

GOOD SOURCE OF
VITAMINS A, C, B$_1$, B$_2$, AND B$_6$, COPPER, POTASSIUM, ZINC, MAGNESIUM, PHOSPHORUS, IRON, AND CALCIUM

Cheerful monkey

A great, refreshing pick-me-up. Papaya is a good source of vitamin C, beta-carotene, the plant form of vitamin A, and the enzyme papain, which aids digestion in the body. A glass of this will keep your cheerful monkeys full of energy and assist healthy development. One (14-ounce) can of apricot halves in natural juice can be used instead of the papaya and apple juice for a convenient pantry version.

Ingredients

- 1 papaya
- 1 banana
- 1 orange
- 1¼ cups apple juice

GOOD SOURCE OF
VITAMINS A AND C,
CALCIUM, POTASSIUM,
MAGNESIUM,
AND IRON

1 Halve and seed the papaya, then scoop out the flesh with a spoon and put it into a blender.

2 Peel and slice the banana and peel and segment the orange, then put them into the blender with the apple juice and a couple of ice cubes.

3 Blend until smooth and serve.

Witches brew

A creamy smoothie that is a meal in itself, this is an excellent choice for a recuperating child because avocados are considered a complete food that is easy to digest. When combined with banana and milk, they make a great fuel for growth and repair.

Ingredients

- 1 small ripe avocado
- 1 small ripe banana
- 1 cup skim milk

1 Peel and pit the avocado, then peel the banana.

2 Put the avocado, banana, and milk into a blender and blend until smooth.

3 Pour into glasses, add a couple of ice cubes, and serve immediately.

GOOD SOURCE OF
VITAMINS C, E, B_1, B_2, B_6, AND B_{12}, FOLIC ACID, CALCIUM, POTASSIUM, COPPER, ZINC, MAGNESIUM, AND PHOSPHORUS

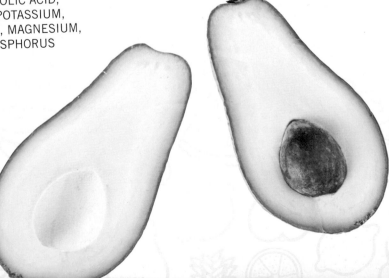

Peaches and cream

MAKES 1 standard glass ···········

This winning combination can easily be adapted to a pantry version using canned peaches or apricots, or you can substitute nectarines for the peaches if they are more readily available. It's a great way to add calcium to the diet of a child who isn't very enthusiastic about eating their greens.

Ingredients
- 1 large peach
- ⅔ cup plain yogurt
- ¼ cup milk
- a few raspberries, to garnish

1 Peel the peach, remove the pit, and coarsely chop the flesh.

2 Put the peach, yogurt, and milk into a blender and blend until smooth.

3 Garnish with raspberries.

GOOD SOURCE OF
VITAMIN C, BETA-CAROTENE, AND ZINC

Supershaker

If your child is aching from head to toe and can't seem to function, you need to replace vital potassium and get some vitamin c into their system. They would also probably benefit from some extra B vitamins. This fruity smoothie delivers on all three counts and will help an overburdened immune system.

Ingredients

- 4 ounces strawberries (about 1 cup prepared)
- ⅓ pineapple
- 1 banana

GOOD SOURCE OF
VITAMINS C AND B, MAGNESIUM, POTASSIUM, AND ZINC

1 Hull the strawberries. Peel the pineapple, remove the core in the center, and coarsely chop the flesh.

2 Juice the two fruits (reserving strawberries to garnish), then pour the juice into a blender, add the banana and a couple of ice cubes, and blend until smooth.

3 Serve garnished with strawberries.

Sleeping beauty

If your child is overexcited or anxious and can't sleep, a delicious smoothie at bedtime should help. Soy milk and almonds are both high in tryptophan. This is converted in the body into the brain chemical serotonin, which alleviates insomnia, calms nerves, and helps relaxation. This juice is also high in magnesium and vitamin c, making it a good booster for the adrenal glands and immune system.

Ingredients

- 4 ounces fresh or frozen strawberries (about 1 cup prepared)
- 1 cup soy milk
- 2 kiwifruits
- ¼ cup slivered almonds (optional)

1 Hull the strawberries. Put all the ingredients into a blender. If using fresh instead of frozen strawberries, add a few ice cubes, then blend until smooth.

2 Pour into a glass and garnish with slivered almonds, if desired.

GOOD SOURCE OF
VITAMINS C AND E, ZINC,
TRYPTOPHAN, CALCIUM,
AND MAGNESIUM

Chocolate heaven

·········· **MAKES** 2 standard glasses ··········

This should keep any requests for additive-ridden, sugary thick shakes at bay. It's not the healthiest snack, but a lot healthier than the fast-food versions.

Ingredients

- 1 banana
- 2 tablespoons organic unsweetened cocoa powder
- 1¼ cups low-fat milk
- ½ cup apple juice
- 2 large scoops vanilla ice cream
- chocolate shavings to garnish (optional)

GOOD SOURCE OF
VITAMIN C, CALCIUM, POTASSIUM, TRYPTOPHAN, AND MAGNESIUM

1 Peel and coarsely chop the banana.

2 Put everything into a blender and blend.

3 Pour into glasses and dust with cocoa powder or chocolate shavings.

Jungle fever

Bananas and mangoes both supply fiber, making this a filling and satisfying smoothie that provides a good source of carbohydrate to fuel activity and refuel afterward. The yogurt is a good source of calcium, which is essential for bone health and strength.

Ingredients
- 1 large banana
- 1 large ripe mango
- ⅔ cup plain yogurt
- 1¼ cups pineapple juice

1 Peel and slice the banana, then put it into a freezer container and freeze for at least 2 hours or overnight.

2 Peel the mango, remove the pit, and cube the flesh.

3 Put the frozen banana, mango, yogurt, and pineapple juice into a blender.

4 Blend until smooth and serve immediately, garnished with a slice of banana, if desired.

GOOD SOURCE OF
VITAMINS A, C, B_1, B_2, AND B_6,
FOLIC ACID, CALCIUM,
POTASSIUM, COPPER,
MAGNESIUM, AND PHOSPHORUS

GOOD SOURCE OF
VITAMINS A, C, B_1, B_2, AND B_6,
FOLIC ACID, POTASSIUM, COPPER,
MAGNESIUM, AND PHOSPHORUS

Bionic tonic

A great all-around smoothie—this is easily absorbed and provides a good energy boost. The bananas and mangoes supply essential fiber, and adding yogurt is an effective way to increase the calcium content, which is essential for bone health and strength—truly a bionic tonic.

Ingredients

- 1 small banana
- ½ large ripe mango
- ⅓ cup plain yogurt
- ⅔ cup pineapple juice
- pineapple chunks to garnish (optional)

1 Peel and slice the banana, then put it into a freezer container for at least 2 hours or overnight. Peel the mango, remove the pit, and coarsely chop the flesh.

2 Put the mango into a blender with the frozen banana, yogurt, and pineapple juice.

3 Blend until smooth and serve immediately, garnished with pineapple chunks, if desired.

Index

ACKNOWLEDGMENTS

The publishers would like to thank
Kiara, Michaela, Ellen, Samuel, Charlotte,
Daisy, Joshua, Martha, Willoughby, Ellie, Milly,
Avni, Charlie, Sam, Ines, Elliot, Frazer,
Scarlett, Elsie, Annie, Jack, and Imogen
for being such wonderful models.

CONSULTANT PUBLISHER: Sarah Ford
EDITORIAL ASSISTANT: Meri Pentikäinen
DESIGN: Eoghan O'Brien and Clare Barber
PHOTOGRAPHER: Vanessa Davies
STYLIST: Marianne De Vries
HOME ECONOMISTS: Cara Hobday and Katie Bishop
PRODUCTION CONTROLLER: Sarah-Jayne Johnson